PATRIOTIC SYMBOLS

Mount Rushmore

Nancy Harris

Heinemann Library
Chicago, Illinois

HEINEMANN-RAINTREE

TO ORDER:

☎ Phone Customer Service **888-454-2279**

💻 Visit **www.heinemannraintree.com** to browse our catalog and order online.

Editorial: Rebecca Rissman
Design: Kimberly R. Miracle
Photo Research: Tracy Cummins and Heather Mauldin
Production: Duncan Gilbert

Originated by Dot Gradations
Printed and bound in China by South China Printing Co. Ltd.
The paper used to print this book comes from sustainable resources.

ISBN-13: 978-1-4329-0964-2 (hc)
ISBN-10: 1-4329-0964-9 (hc)
ISBN-13: 978-1-4329-0971-0 (pb)
ISBN-10: 1-4329-0971-1 (pb)

12 11 10 09 08
10 9 8 7 6 5 4 3 2 1

Cataloging-in-Publication data avaiable at Library of Congress:loc.gov

Acknowledgments
The author and publisher are grateful to the following for permission to reproduce copyright material: ©Age Fotostock **p. 5** top left (Maurizio Borsari); ©Associated Press **p. 11**; ©Corbis **pp. 19, 23b** (Underwood & Underwood); ©Getty Images **p. 6** (Ted Wood); ©The Granger Collection, New York **pp. 12, 14, 23c**; ©Library of Congress Prints and Photographs Division **pp. 16, 18, 21** all; ©photos.com **p. 10**; ©Shutterstock **pp. 4** (Raymond Kasprzak), **5** top right (Arvind Balaraman), **5** bottom right (Stephen Finn), **5** bottom left (ExaMedia Photography), **7, 23a** (Jamie Cross), **8**; ©SuperStock, Inc. **p. 17** (SuperStock).

Cover image used with permission of ©Jupiter Images (Corbis/Visions of America/Joseph Sohm). Back cover image used with permission of ©Shutterstock (Raymond Kasprzak).

The publishers would like to thank Nancy Harris for her assistance in the preparation of this book.

Every effort has been made to contact copyright holders of any material reproduced in this book. Any omissions will be rectified in subsequent printings if notice is given to the publisher.

Contents

What Is a Symbol?

Mount Rushmore is a symbol.

A symbol is a type of sign.

A symbol shows you something.

Mount Rushmore

Mount Rushmore is a special symbol.

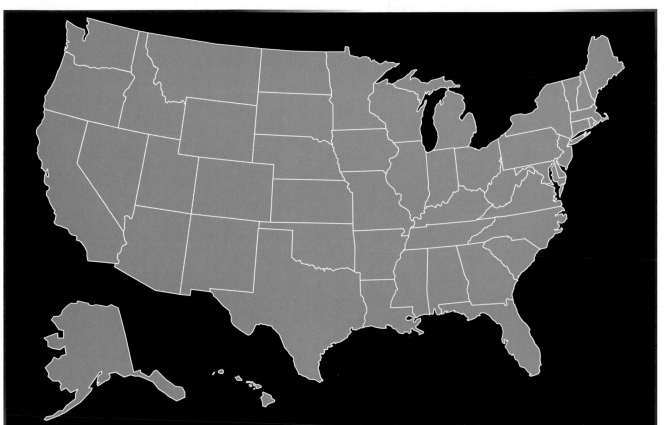

It is a symbol of the United States of America.
The United States of America is a country.

Mount Rushmore is a patriotic symbol.

NEW HAMPSHIRE
MASSACHUSETTS
NEW YORK
RHODE ISLAND
PENNSYLVANIA
CONNECTICUT
NEW JERSEY
DELAWARE
MARYLAND
VIRGINIA
NORTH CAROLINA
SOUTH CAROLINA
GEORGIA

1775

It shows the beliefs of the country.
It shows the history of the country.

Presidents

George Washington

Thomas Jefferson

Theodore Roosevelt

Abraham Lincoln

Mount Rushmore is a sculpture. It shows the faces of four United States presidents.

President
John F. Kennedy

The president is the leader of a country.

George Washington

George Washington was the first president. He helped fight to make the United States a new country.

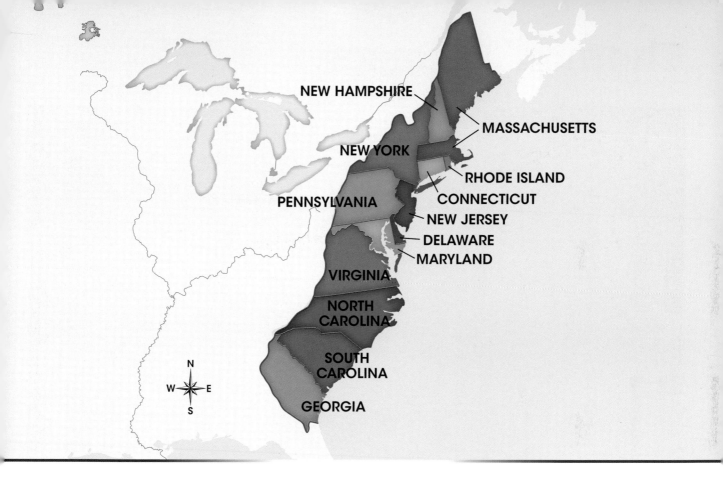

He is a symbol of the beginning of the new country.

Thomas Jefferson

Thomas Jefferson was the third president. He helped get more land for the country.

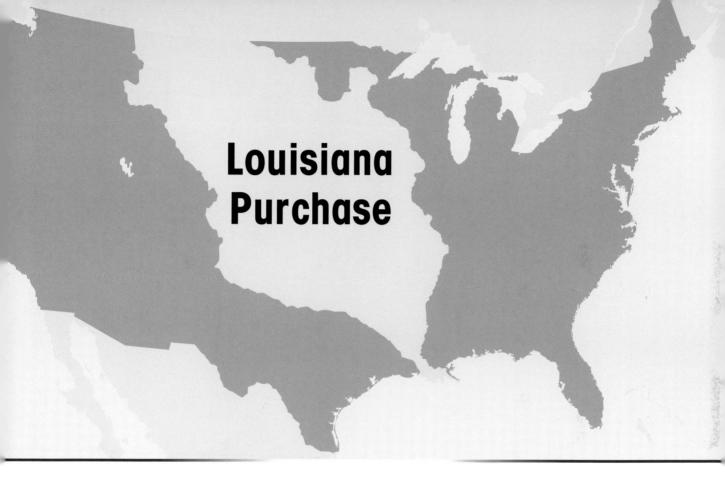

Louisiana Purchase

He is a symbol of how the country grew larger over time.

Abraham Lincoln

Abraham Lincoln was the 16th president. He helped make all people free in the country.

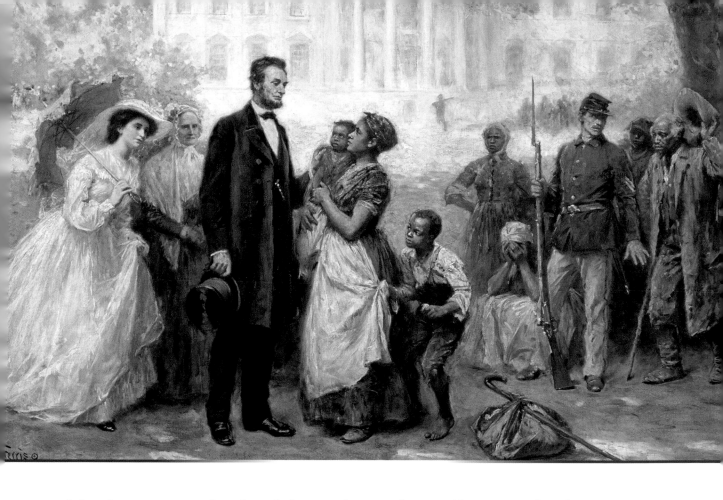

He is a symbol of freedom for all people in the United States.

Theodore Roosevelt

Theodore Roosevelt was the 26th president. He helped make the United States a strong country.

President Roosevelt

World Leaders

He is a symbol of how the United States became a powerful country.

What It Tells You

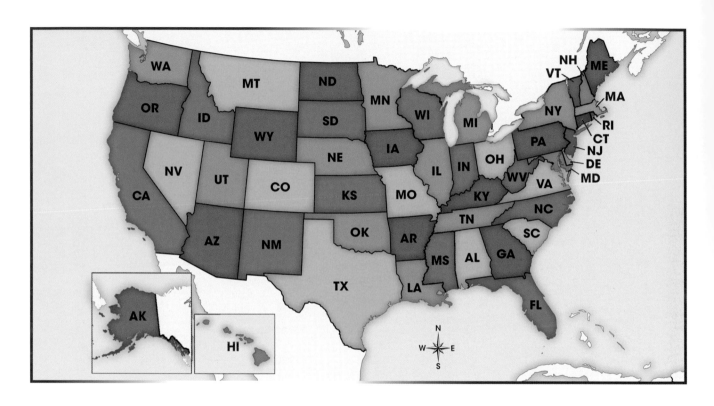

Mount Rushmore tells you how the United States grew over time.

George Washington

Abraham Lincoln

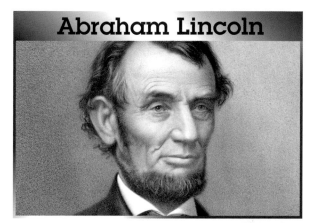

Thomas Jefferson

Theodore Roosevelt

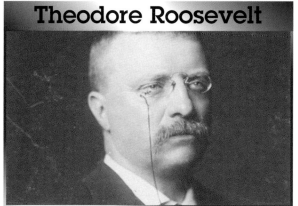

It shows how our leaders helped to make a strong country.

Mount Rushmore Facts

★ Mount Rushmore is in the state of South Dakota.

★ It is carved in the Black Hills.

★ Gutzon Borglum and his son Lincoln made the sculpture.

★ Workers helped them.

Glossary

country
area of land governed by the same group

history
what happened in the past

President of the United States
head of the country who is chosen by the people

Index

Note to Parents and Teachers

The study of patriotic symbols introduces young readers to our country's government and history. Books in this series begin by defining a symbol before focusing on the history and significance of a specific patriotic symbol. Use the facts section on page 22 to introduce readers to these non-fiction features.

The text has been carefully chosen with the advice of a literacy expert to enable beginning readers success while reading independently or with moderate support. An expert in the field of early childhood social studies curriculum was consulted to provide interesting and appropriate content.

You can support children's nonfiction literacy skills by helping students use the table of contents, headings, picture glossary, and index.